Quiet Spaces

The brf prayer and spirituality journal

Sit

Edited by Heather Fenton

Published by
The Bible Reading Fellowship
15 The Chambers
Abingdon, OX14 3FE
United Kingdom
Tel: +44 (0)1865 319700
Email: enquiries@brf.org.uk
Website: www.brf.org.uk
BRF is a Registered Charity

ISBN 978 1 84101 832 4
First published 2011
10 9 8 7 6 5 4 3 2 1 0

Acknowledgements
Scripture quotations taken from The Holy Bible, New International Version, copyright © 1973, 1978, 1984 by International Bible Society, are used by permission of Hodder & Stoughton, a member of the Hachette Livre UK Group. All rights reserved. 'NIV' is a registered trademark of International Bible Society. UK trademark number 1448790.

Scripture quotations taken from The Holy Bible, Today's New International Version. Copyright © 2004 by International Bible Society. Used by permission of Hodder & Stoughton, a member of the Hachette Livre UK Group. All rights reserved. 'TNIV' is a registered trademark of International Bible Society.

Scripture quotations taken from The New Revised Standard Version of the Bible, Anglicised Edition, copyright © 1989, 1995 by the Division of Christian Education of the National Council of the Churches of Christ in the USA, and are used by permission. All rights reserved.

Extracts from the Authorised Version of the Bible (The King James Bible), the rights in which are vested in the Crown, are reproduced by permission of the Crown's patentee, Cambridge University Press.

Scripture quotations taken from the Contemporary English Version of the Bible, published by HarperCollins Publishers, are copyright © 1991, 1992, 1995 American Bible Society.

A catalogue record for this book is available from the British Library

Printed in the UK by Rainbow Print

VOLUME 21 Contents

The Editor writes...

Heather Fenton is the Editor of *Quiet Spaces*.

This first of three issues of *Quiet Spaces* is entitled 'Sit' and will be followed by 'Walk' and 'Stand'. As the preparations for the Olympics make us marvel at the possibilities of the human body, so the themes chosen are around these basic postures. The order of the themes comes at least in part from my strong recollections of reading Watchman Nee's spiritual classic *Sit, Walk, Stand*. In this first issue, Tony Horsfall, who has spent a number of years in China, introduces us to the spirituality of Watchman Nee.

Ray Simpson, who has lived on Holy Island for a number of years and knows that many people use the island as a place of retreat, points out that if we wish to be athletes of the Spirit, learning to sit is the best place to begin, and he even gives some sitting exercises to start with. Meanwhile Rachel Thorpe, a young writer new to *Quiet Spaces*, gets excited about the readings in Mark 10 and Revelation about the prospects for being seated with Jesus in his glory.

Gordon Giles, who is a vicar and a musician as well as being a long-term contributor to *Quiet Spaces*, contributes 'Singing with the seated soul'. Gordon points out the differences between hearing music, which we can do while carrying out all sorts of other tasks, and actually listening to it. Listening means paying proper attention, and that probably means sitting down with this as our sole intention, which is quite different!

The title of Rosemary Feuell's article 'Sitting in his shade' is based on the Song of Songs (2:3). Rosemary has strong connections with St Beuno's retreat house in North Wales. She talks of setting our minds on God, enjoying being seated with him, and gives some practical suggestions about how we might do this.

Margaret Harvey reflects on the use of the word 'sit', beginning with remembering her school days and how the tone of voice used was part of the teacher's communication to the class. As I get a bit older and begin to need to sit down more often, I reflect on God's call to Abram. Well into what we may consider 'retirement' time and beyond, he receives an amazing call from God, although he does get some opportunities to sit down!

Liz Pacey has obviously taken time to sit and write the prayers she offers us, while Carol Jerman goes for an exploration of one of David Adam's books. David, who, like Ray Simpson, has spent a lot of time on Holy Island, has written a number of books, including the recently republished *Tides and Seasons: modern prayers in the Celtic tradition* and we are pleased that this is the first book review to be included in *Quiet Spaces*. Together with prayers from John Birch, and a taster of two BRF books, that completes this issue of *Quiet Spaces*. So now it is up to you to find a 'quiet space' and 'sit'!

If you would like to get in touch with me regarding your responses or ideas for future issues of *Quiet Spaces*, please do feel free to contact me. My email address is quietspaces@brf.org.uk or you can write via the BRF offices in Abingdon (see page 2 for the address).

RAY SIMPSON

From where I sit

author

Ray Simpson is Founding Guardian of the international Community of Aidan and Hilda and Principal Tutor of its Celtic Christian Studies programmes. He is a prolific author. He writes a weekly blog (search for 'Ray Simpson blog') and a daily prayer tweet on twitter.com/whitehouseviews. He leads retreats and lectures widely, and lives on the Holy Island of Lindisfarne.

Learning to sit will not qualify us for an Olympic gold medal, although good posture helps. If, however, we wish to be athletes of the Spirit, learning to sit is the best place to begin. Early Christians in our land were excited to holiness by the example of fourth-century desert fathers and mothers who became known as athletes of the Spirit. Abba Ammonas was asked, 'What is the "narrow and hard way"?' (see Matthew 7:14). He replied, 'The narrow and hard way is this, to control your thoughts, and to strip yourself of your own will, for the sake of God.' They were spiritual athletes because they stripped themselves of everything that would hold them back from running towards the divine goal of life. What was that goal? That there would be nothing left but the love that leads to eternal union with God.

Olympic standards are beyond the reach of most us, and we may think that the training required to be God's athlete is also too harsh for us. We would be mistaken. In my book *The Joy of Spiritual Fitness* (Kevin Mayhew, 2010) the exercises are graded. True, they end with the tough power-lifting stuff—'storming the gates of heaven'—but they begin with the most gentle warm-ups. In fact, the first is a sun-bathing exercise as follows:

Sit or lie comfortably. Breathe rhythmically. Imagine you are on a beach. Allow the sun to soak into your skin. Feel it relaxing you until it tingles through your whole body, warming you inside, too. Now focus on the sun above you. But this time let it be the Sun of suns, the uncreated Source of all energy, goodness, affection. Feel the warm rays of Love alighting upon you, filling you. Take time to enjoy these rays of the True Sun. Another time, enjoy different rays that make you feel affirmed, such as rays of peace or wisdom.

Relaxing is a help, but it is not quite the same as stillness, which is a next step. Meister Eckhart said, 'Nothing in all creation is so close to God as stillness.' Stillness is not even the same as silence. Stillness is a way of being, a putting away of frenzied and fearful circuits of the mind, a receptivity to what is, a nestling in the heart of God.

I read in the Bible that 'Jesus would often go to some place where he could be alone and pray' (Luke 5:16, CEV). As he sat, say, on a mountainside boulder, I imagine he first placed into the Father's

Olympic standards are beyond the reach of most us, and we may think that the training required to be God's athlete is also too harsh for us...

Stillness is a way of being

hands the many thoughts and activities that could so easily have taken him over. We call this offloading or chilling out. Some people offload before going to sleep. The apostle Paul urged us not to let the sun go down on our anger (Ephesians 4:26)—or, as I think of it, on too much unsorted primal material. The practice of the Examen—examining our actions and attitudes during the day—is a way of responding to Paul's advice.

One of us will go down from our seat and do the washing-up for someone, because that is the act of love that brings heaven to earth at that moment

We ask forgiveness for mistakes, we give thanks for 'good flow'; we learn from both, and we place all into God's lap.

After Jesus offloaded, what did he focus on next as he sat on that mountainside? He had choices: should he respond to the urgent call of a grieving family (for example, Mary and Martha), heal the sick on his doorstep, or train his disciples? Should he stay in Galilee or go to Jerusalem now, or later, or never? We, too, are bombarded with pressures. We suffer from data overload and choice fatigue. Our desire to live for God is hijacked by a world and sometimes by a church that makes much ado about nothing.

As we sit, like Jesus on that mountainside, familiar roads cross our minds, but also a road less travelled. How do we discern which road we should follow? We use this precious sitting time to review everything down below, on earth, in the light of eternity's priorities. Because God has made each of us so different, the priorities will vary much. One of us will go down from our seat and do the washing-up for someone, because that is the act of love that brings heaven to earth at that moment. Others of us will wait longer until something that we were put on earth for, but which has not yet come to birth, crystallises in our minds. 'Silence is the element in which great things fashion themselves,' wrote Thomas Carlyle (1795–1881). In silence we begin to access the 'electronics' of the Spirit, whereby a thought from the Author of mind can slip into our minds. Such spiritual information gives us a sense of perspective, courage and inspiration. Though it may well re-awaken a dormant conscience, it is more than that. The Italian poet Rosa Bellino suggests that silence is 'the womb, the space, that allows one to hear "a harmony and a rhythm"'. We become like children, and we enter the kingdom of God.

Sit with God on the internet?

The Olympics have become globalised. *New York Times* journalist Thomas Friedman writes in his book *The Lexus and the Olive Tree* (HarperCollins, 2000) that one of the characteristics of globalisation is 'super-empowered individuals who are enabled to enlist others around a cause through information technology'. He identifies six dimensions of globalisation but misses out the most significant—the spiritual.

Sitting with God on the internet? I facilitated a group workshop with this title. At first we were dismissive of the internet. We thought it was a distraction from the true spiritual path because it majored on froth generated by ego-

> We ask forgiveness
> for mistakes,
> we give thanks
> for 'good flow';
> we learn from both...

centred people. I vowed I would never do Twitter. Then, we asked whether God could redeem the internet. Could it be an instrument of people who transcend the ego and live in the world of the Spirit? Shortly afterwards I did an Enneagram course. I was dismayed to find that I was a Number Four. At their worst, these wallow in introspective self-pity. Redeemed Number Fours, however, reach out to others, ideally to the whole world. That was when, in a flash, I knew I should do Twitter.

What should I Tweet? I thought of the Bible. Is not the book of Proverbs something like that? People spoke pithy sayings for anyone who bothered to listen. The most memorable were collected. From these collections a selection was made—and we have our book of Proverbs. In modern terms it could be called 'The book of Tweets'.

My home on Holy Island is named White House. The friend who set up my Twitter account gave it the username @whitehouseviews. When I searched for this, I found myself next to President Obama, but he had hundreds of thousands of followers and I had one! I tried the 'sitting prayer of stillness' and heard the birds. I thought: 'The birds often tweet for pure joy, with no ulterior motive. Why don't I Tweet for pure joy? Why not start the day with one Tweet that comes as I sit in God's presence? This is valid whether many or none are listening.' My first such Tweet was: 'May I tweet with the melody of the lark, the wisdom of the owl, the energy of the wild goose, in the name of the Holy Dove.'

I am blessed. At 8 a.m. each day on Holy Island someone gives a homily that applies the day's Gospel reading to us. Sometimes a sentence from this becomes my Tweet: the world can now eavesdrop on a Holy Island homily. At other times a stream of communications flows through my laptop from emailers or resource material and something from this becomes the Tweet. The laptop is on a desk that has my White House views. An inspiration pops into my head from the perspective of the places I look upon. I see Farne Isle, where Saint Cuthbert stormed the gates of heaven; Bamburgh Rock, whence Saint Aidan went to heaven escorted by angels; and Holy Island, to which countless pilgrims come to seek God. Now a daily prayer Tweet and a weekly blog are a natural part of my intentional rhythm of prayer, work and recreation. 'Liquid church' can make unprecedented waves through the internet.

> The world can now eavesdrop on a Holy Island homily

Listening

Visitors come and they, too, take time to sit. One of them informs me: 'I'm taking time to let what's buried beneath the flotsam rise to the surface.' A pastor tells me that on his first visit he strode quickly through the field of sheep in the way he walks around his parish, and the sheep scattered. On his second visit he sat quietly on a bench and the sheep gathered round him. He felt that was a living parable through which God spoke. His human flock would gather round if he learned to be still.

As we learn to sit we also gather those fragments of memory that stand out like sentinels of heaven's kingdom. At the age of 13 I became a Christian. Three years later I nearly became an atheist. Why? The people I read about in the Bible listened to God—the Christians I knew did not. Communists in those days had a passion, a philosophy and plan to change the world without God, and certain Bible heroes had a passion, philosophy and plan to change their world with God. The Christians I knew merely told people, 'All you need is Jesus,' failing to take into account that Jesus said, 'You have ears—why don't you listen?' Then I met some Christians who did listen. They used to say, 'God gave us two ears and one mouth—why don't we listen twice as much as we talk?' That set me on a lifelong quest to discover the art of listening. I found that this faculty has become a victim of endless soundbites that don't come from God, and of capitalism's 'hidden persuaders' who misinform our unconscious thinking in order to sell their products. The biblical story of Samuel, however, gave me hope. For he also grew up in a society in which listening was a lost art. I reflect that the problem is not that God stops speaking, but that we no longer recognise God's voice; the Samuel experience was a turning point in a nation, and it can be a turning point for us.

As I sit I recall a friend who thought that my arrogant attempts to listen to

As we learn to sit we also gather those fragments of memory that stand out like sentinels of heaven's kingdom

God for big things blanked out God's voice in little things. She emailed me the following well-known piece (author unknown):

The man whispered, 'God speak to me,'
and a meadowlark sang.
But the man did not hear.
So the man yelled, 'God speak to me,'
and the thunder rolled across the sky.
But the man did not listen.
The man looked around and said,
'God show me a miracle!' and new
life was born.

> The problem is not that God stops speaking, but that **we no longer recognise God's voice...**

But the man did not know.
So the man cried out in despair, 'Touch
me, God, and let me know you are
here!' whereupon God reached down
and touched the man.
But the man brushed the butterfly away
and walked on.

As I sit I recall a version of Psalm 58. It refers to 'the deaf adder that stoppeth her ears; which will not hearken the voice of the charmers, charming never so wisely' (vv. 4–5, KJV). The psalmist singles out unwillingness to listen as the epitome of wickedness. It is not hard to see why. To stop one's ears against someone is to deny that they are the neighbour whom we are commanded to love. To stop our ears against God is even more harmful.

As I sit I sense the importance of tuning in to the unseen currents that shape our lives and civilisation. This is understood by those who are in touch with their intuition. Some Christians fear or denounce this use of intuition. They have a point, for it may be better to be deaf than to listen to falsehood—but why should the devil have all the best ears? Celtic and other saints reassure us that it is possible for Christians to develop intuitive powers, as did Jesus, in a way that attunes them only to the Father's wavelength. Jesus only did what he saw his Father doing (John 5:19) and we can do likewise (14:12).

'Make me aware, dear God, of the universe within, and of the beatings of your heart' (Ray Simpson, *Waymarks for the Journey: Daily prayer to change your world*, Kevin Mayhew, 2009).

ROSEY FEUELL

Sitting in his shade

'Sit with this awhile,' said my tutor. 'Come and sit beside me,' a dying friend asked in his lovely Derbyshire garden. 'Sit and think it over,' the solicitor suggested. Each time the hint to linger, take one's time, enjoy another person's company or savour important thoughts. Easy words to say, hard ones to obey. We are impatient for action and achievement, while lacking focus of mind and heart to enable those things to happen. We prefer to run before walking, and will walk anywhere before agreeing to sit and sift our desires or turmoil.

Sitting has special significance in the Bible. It can be a triumphant end to effort: we are already 'seated with him [Christ] in the heavenly realms' (Ephesians 2:6, NIV). It is a feature of personal behaviour, known intimately only to God: 'You know when I sit and when I rise' (Psalm 139:2). It denotes slightly aimless waiting, like 'children sitting in the marketplace' (Matthew 11:16), or Mary Magdalene and the

author

Rosey Feuell is a semi-retired teacher offering spiritual direction, Christian and neighbourhood events and Quiet Days in Cambridge area. Her interests include poetry, walking, swimming, reading and travel.

other Mary 'sitting... opposite the tomb' (27:61) as Jesus is buried. God 'sits enthroned above the circle of the earth' (Isaiah 40:22), supportively supreme, but when humans sit, it can represent judgment or scorn: 'Blessed is the man who does not... sit in the seat of mockers' (Psalm 1:1). One may sit 'in darkness and the deepest gloom' (107:10), as did Job, seeking consolation in suffering. Thus sitting, just lingering in places or emotions, can indicate abandonment of hope.

Common to all these scriptural 'sittings' is that Creator or creature has ceased from frenetic striving for success. Sitting means taking a position and waiting, as oneself or in appointed roles: on the throne, 'in the gateway' (as arbiter—see 2 Samuel 19:8), in expectancy or openness towards what might arise. One is no longer driven to be or do something, but is simply present, reminiscent of Shakespeare in *King Lear*: 'The wheel is come full circle: I am here.'

... we are usually tempted to try action first, rather than sitting

Stillness is paramount

Stillness is paramount—acceptance and rest, not sleep, are key. Yet this isn't natural to us. Chaotic, spontaneous or organised, we are usually tempted to try action first, rather than sitting: tackle chores, phone the first available friend, buy sweets. Without such opportunities, we make a drink, go into the garden or pick up a magazine. This is always easier than sitting with thoughts, struggling to pray, or facing inner poverty and powerlessness. Of course we care about people and things in our lives and want to manage them. It is possible to care too much, and to miss the real way to appreciate.

We interfere too much. It is hard to stay, perplexed, seeking—or being surprised by—the peace our Lord intends for us amid maybe demanding circumstances.

Sometimes it takes tragedy or crises to open this dimension. The mechanics

The first retreat was fairly mixed: **unwinding was slow initially**

© St Beuno's Retreat Centre

may be very simple, although persevering in sitting is more exacting. This applies throughout life; quiet reflection (usually skipped) benefits almost all activities or decisions. So it is with new departures, however joyful. I recall the Russian custom of sitting down with one's travelling companions in a room with doors shut, bags packed, before starting the journey. Trust must be sought for the transition.

How much more powerful these imperatives in our life journey with Jesus! We admit difficulty with sitting and thinking generally: 'too busy', 'too depressing', 'wasting time' and so on, we say. When it comes to prayer, almost everyone looks embarrassed, confesses they don't pray as much as they should, or explains that outside church, problems or danger, they hardly pray at all. Reasons for not cultivating our times with God are predictable, but counter-productive, since we gain only by opening ourselves fully to our Lord, sitting quietly with him regularly.

Honest people may that concede this avoidance is pathetic… few of us fight the trend and pass on winning tips. Perhaps we sense that such insights are hard-hitting, unwelcome, or think they

> Reasons for not cultivating our times with God are predictable, but **counter-productive…**

> Grimly I realised **I could not take more discussions**

belong to priests or spiritual directors.

Personally I would like to share how renewing and transforming I have found experiences of simply sitting. By this I mean sitting with God, giving him time to enter my life, to fill my prayers and my head with understanding of him, his work in me and the world. This can be sitting spontaneously over coffee, or part of planned prayer or holiday. The journey has been fruitful, with both short-term and longer-term overwhelming and sharpening awareness of his love and deep knowledge of me. The tree planted by water feels delicious inflowing, life-giving moisture; the same tree, later, in drought, is able to draw on those moisture reserves in veins and core.

My early life was low on affirmation and encouragement. When I found Christ, he seemed to feed that nourishment back in various ways as I matured: through Christian worship, scripture, fellowship and likewise through study, unlikely friends, travel and creation itself. I was like a puppy, eager, able to recognise what ministered to growth, and leave debatable possibilities. Later I had some prayer ministry, bringing my hurts and limitations to Christ for his gentle healing touch. Eventually those who had prayed for me suggested I wasn't making progress and repeatedly tracked similar ground. Instantly I saw why: they prayed with me, for me, and I prayed right there, then zoomed to my busy life—where inevitably I postponed introspection about what had happened and the new space I could be in.

Possible remedies were counselling or attending different 'healing' groups. Grimly I realised I could not take more discussions, imposed insights or meetings, nor did I have the energy or time, nor could I manage the travelling involved. I already did a 50-hour week and professional weekend work to meet the mortgage. Improvement had to be 'quality', not quantity! Old ideas returned: go on retreat, find time to pray there. No intermediaries, phone calls, buoying oneself up by lyrics or fellowship. Just sitting there, with God—asking him to work in what I could work out and overall show me his love for my woundedness, his wisdom for life's difficulties. My counsellors were surprised and dismissive. After three months, nevertheless, I announced my agenda: 'retreats until further notice'. That was 17 years ago.

The first retreat was fairly mixed: unwinding was slow initially, as I had foolishly taken unfinished academic work, but blissful times came, simply to sit pondering the retreat guide's scriptures, sharing my heart's responses with the Lord. Soon I found delights unfolded, ancient truths coming home to me freshly, as I sat in the apple orchard, walked the Downs or took time over tea in my plain, comfy bedroom over the garden. Many everyday things cheered me too as I had leisure to observe and absorb them.

One evening, below the wide windows of my room, someone emerged from luxuriant flower beds below. There was a sense of recognition: a Sister of this order, someone whose vitality I had seen at sacred dance years ago. She also resembled the 'favourite auntie' of my life—and here she was again, offering vigorous reminders of the beautiful support figures and joyful experiences given to me. Visitors suddenly stole across the dusky lawn towards Sister Mona; her greeting was to reach out to the most intricate fragrant shrub, her face, and soon theirs, alive with wonder

Soon I found delights unfolded, ancient truths coming home to me freshly...

It became perfectly natural, addictive and **hard to leave**

at the plant's sheer exuberance. It was very simple, profoundly exciting. I was sitting in the Lord's shade, upstairs, tasting sweet ways in which he was developing my sense of his love, his faithful concern for me, through my puzzling, precious life.

I had many such retreats, meeting Jesus in scripture, sensing his presence and life's coherence more vividly as I strolled. These intimations poured on into daily life and its stressful situations, where I often felt like a snared bird or a creature stumbling into nets. Sometimes it was harder to sit still, at other times it became perfectly natural, addictive and hard to leave. Whatever happened around me, there was a sense of growing and deepening: Christ of Galilee was here, nurturing me onwards.

Need for confirmation in my new perceptions led me to ongoing spiritual direction in my home area. I also discovered that language may be unequal to expressing what one has experienced in all this sitting with God. That became less important, though, alongside the reality that I had 'own space' with Jesus, where I could easily return for shelter and empowering. Similarly I became more enthusiastic about using the Bible when bedding down, wanting to involve imagination and emotions more fully in my prayer. I am no artist, but in earlier retreats I had relished sketching country scenes and stencilling creaturely shapes: starfish, seashells, cheery birds. Suddenly it mattered to be more holistic in registering what I saw and felt as I sat.

The poet Gerard Manley Hopkins (1844–89) always draws me with his 'As kingfishers catch fire' and attention to 'the dearest freshness deep down things' ('God's Grandeur'). The unevenness of his experience resonates with me: 'I greet Him the days I meet Him and bless when I understand' ('Wreck of the Deutschland'). When I discovered from a spiritual director that there were retreats in the very house where Hopkins flourished, I sat with it longingly for two years: a big house, a long way from Cambridge, Ignatian contemplation! Too overwhelming? Overcrowded? Offputting? Largely for initiates? Odd for Anglicans? I had enjoyed sitting with God by the sea, in forests, at home with tea and toast, and was not sure.

Suddenly clarity came: 'Make a booking for St Beuno's. Go for it! Say you are new to things.' And I did. Trembling, I took trains to North Wales and checked in. I was over the rose garden and could immediately see many lovely places to sit. It was welcoming, and kind, 'a house where all were good to me' ('In the Valley of the Elwy'), even to cooking another breakfast when I came down late and found mine gone. There was an art room, silence, space. My retreat guide appeared in *The Big Silence* on TV in 2010: I would not have been surprised to learn this then!

More enthusiastic about using the Bible when bedding down...

I discovered what can happen to your whole **self-awareness**

> They were delightful times

The first night, fleetingly feeling strange and adrift, I began to be very deeply at home. I wept, knowing that God was desirous of meeting me in the weariness of this uncertain time, between the deaths of my two parents. 'Jeni' taught me to centre myself in scripture, enter the narrative and use a whole array of paintings for reflection too. I spent time sitting with my thoughts, frustrations, yearnings for God to touch me. I climbed the hills and surveyed the Vale of Clwyd, sat in shadows as well as sun... glimpsed the distant sea, backed by Great Orme and Snowdon. In relationship with my Creator too I had a vista of possibilities: recollections of struggling uphill, visions of beauty, moments of challenge, joy of new discoveries in the waters of life. I learnt as well about forgiving myself, releasing my focus on miseries. Like Ezekiel by the Kebar River, I sat about eight days overwhelmed, no longer by bitterness but by truth: my life—sitting, rising, lying—was in God's hands; he held me entirely even when I held him only lightly. They were delightful times sitting in his shadow, knowing his arms underneath. The secret of those 'hidden things' is with me still.

The invitation was to sit. In the end, when I set my mind and especially heart to it, I sat a long time... I discovered what can happen to your whole self-awareness once you explore your life from the perspective of being seated with Christ. This is the most sustaining—indeed the only—way to become ready to walk on and stand your ground in the life he is opening—not closing!—ahead of you. Sitting in his shade creates singing at your work in his garden. It offers us a 'landscape of adoration', as Sister Wendy Beckett has said.

RACHEL THORPE

Save me a seat

'I remember the way that we would celebrate Easter Sunday. Everyone would wear their new outfits and we would colour eggs. The congregation would form a circular procession in the streets, walking and carrying candles and singing. It was so beautiful that it would make the older women weep.'

author

Rachel Thorpe writes about culture, art and faith for magazines, newspapers and blogs. In 2009–10 she was the intern at Christian Heritage, Cambridge.

Helen grew up attending a Macedonian church. Her recollections of her time there form a vivid poetry of colour and sounds. The thing that she remembers most strongly of all? The fact that after the Easter parade her young feet were tired. She would search for somewhere to sit down, but there were no pews in the church, no ledges or recesses. So she would hop from foot to foot while she lit her candles.

It was so beautiful that it would make the older women weep

My memories of growing up in a small Anglican church are quite different. As teenagers, my friends and I always had somewhere to sit. We had claimed the pew at the very back of the church on the left-hand side. It was our spot, special not because of its position but because we had chosen it for ourselves. For almost ten years we sat together in that same pew. Even when the youth group swelled to almost five times its original size, we would cram more people into the creaking wooden frame.

> For almost ten years we sat **together in that same pew**

Last year the church decided to replace the pews with chairs, but by that time the back pew on the left-hand side had a special place in people's hearts. Teenagers are a breed perhaps rarely found in many churches today, but it was different in ours. And people knew where to find us—squashed into the familiar spot that we had chosen. When the pews were removed, my mother, the youth leader, rescued the one that had been ours. It is now happily retired in my parents' back garden, where it has a new life as a bench for sunny days. You can guess where my friends and I choose to sit when we go back to visit.

The particulars of where we chose to park our posteriors may seem a triviality, but they can radically alter our experience and memory of a place, a community or an event. And we are not the only ones to mark its meaning. King David knows this when he writes: 'You know when I sit and when I rise; you perceive my thoughts from afar' (Psalm 139:2, NIV). God knows not only where we sit and what we reflect on; he is with us when we do so, wherever that may be. He was with the Israelites when they sat down by the rivers of Babylon and wept with the memory of their homeland. He was with Jonah when he sat down in the heat to watch what would happen to Nineveh. He was with Mary when she sat enthralled at the feet of Jesus. He is with you now as you sit, reflecting on him.

It may be that you have a particular place where you like to meet with God. For one of my friends it is a battered armchair in her kitchen reserved specifically for Bible reading and prayer. For another it's over an early morning coffee at the dining table. For me it is less of a routine, but I often hear God most

clearly when sitting outside under a tree and gazing up through the leaves. It's only human to want to choose a special spot to meet with someone you love.

The story shows that remarkable faith is not immune from fault

Truly, I say to you

In fact, the Bible contains the account of two young 'sons of thunder' who were very eager to find the perfect spot to sit with Jesus. They wanted to secure themselves the best seats not here on earth but in the life to come. The account in Mark 10 puts the crucial question in the mouths of James and John, whereas Matthew 20 attributes it to their mother. The request itself remains the same: 'Let one of us sit at your right and the other at your left in your glory' (Mark 10:37). James and John are looking to secure the details of a promise that Jesus made a little earlier: 'Truly, I say to you, in the new world, when the Son of Man will sit on his glorious throne, you who have followed me will also sit on twelve thrones, judging the twelve tribes of Israel' (Matthew 19:28, NRSV).

This in turn fulfils the prophecy that the angel Gabriel spoke over Jesus at the time of the annunciation, in which he declared that the infant king would one day sit on David's throne to rule over an eternal kingdom: 'He will be great, and will be called the Son of the Most High; and the Lord God will give him the throne of his ancestor David. He will reign over the house of Jacob forever, and of his kingdom there will be no end' (Luke 1:32–33).

James and John's request proves that they have recognised who Jesus is—the Messiah, the Son of the Highest. They believe that they will one day see Jesus seated in glory, and they want a front row seat! The standard approach of commentators is to assume that their request is wholly inappropriate—after all, Jesus rebukes them for it. But in at least one sense, it is commendable; they have faith in Jesus' identity and destiny. They've seen him transfigured and trust that his statements about the future are true and will come to pass.

Nor is their request deplorably

undemocratic. After all, it's Jesus who makes it clear that some of his followers will be given superior positions of authority and power; VIP seating will be reserved. But Jesus knows that James and John, in their human weakness, have been seduced by the idea of power and rank. After all, it's an attractive image: reigning in judgment over the rest of creation. It's easy to see how their logic may have run. If anyone is worthy of sitting alongside the king of heaven on one of the twelve reserved thrones, it is James and John, core members of his group of disciples. Some commentators even argue that they are his cousins, their mother Salome being the sister of Mary. Shouldn't they sit by his side?

As John Calvin (1509–64) comments, the story shows that remarkable faith is not immune from fault. He writes, '[this story] shows that proper and holy zeal is often accompanied by ambition' (*Calvin's Commentaries*, Vol. 32: Matthew, Mark and Luke, Part II, translated by John King, accessed at www.sacred-texts.com). Jesus is quick to rebuke this desire for prestige. In his kingdom, the God of heaven becomes a servant, washing the feet of his disciples, and his followers must learn to be humbled to the same degree. As he puts it, it is only through the cup of suffering that triumphant glory will come.

When the children sit on the thrones of the kingdom, peace will be restored...

At Cair Paravel in throne

The biblical image of final glory, with Jesus and his followers securely seated on their thrones, appears reflected in C.S. Lewis' book *The Lion, The Witch and the Wardrobe* (HarperCollins, various editions). During the tyrannical reign of the White Witch, the four Pevensie children come to Narnia. The animals who live there explain their ancient saying: 'When Adam's flesh and Adam's bone sit at Cair Paravel in throne, the evil time will be over and done.'

When the children sit on the thrones of the kingdom, peace will be restored. Lewis was reflecting a heavenly reality. When Jesus and his followers are seated on their heavenly thrones, complete peace will be restored as final justice is achieved.

When Jesus and his followers are seated on their heavenly thrones, complete peace will be restored

Let us pause for a moment

At the climax of *The Lion, The Witch and The Wardrobe*, the children do indeed take their seats in a ceremony that is at once 'solemn' and full of 'revelry' and 'rejoicing'. In the recent film adaptation there is a regal sincerity to the proceedings. The children enter, accompanied by the lion Aslan, and as they are seated he turns to introduce them, by name, to the gathered crowds. The biblical parallels are kept close to the surface; not only is he calling them by name and claiming them as his own (see Isaiah 43:1), but he also gives them new names, calling out their worthy characteristics.

Later in the evening, Aslan slips away quietly from the feast. The children may be the new kings and queens of Narnia, but he remains the powerful, mysterious and supreme ruler, Aslan the Good. Yet it is deeply important that he is present at the start, as the one to lead them to their thrones and to introduce them.

Take a seat

Why do I say that it is deeply important? In our fast-paced world we rarely take the time to sit down and rest. When we do, it comes with a set of social customs and linguistic rules. Let us pause for a moment to think about the ways in which we speak about sitting down. You might suggest someone 'has a sit-down', if you are concerned about them and hope that they will take a rest and put their feet up. If you are the kind of person who has a dog, you might tell it to 'sit' when you want it to stay still and behave. You might be polite and offer someone the chance to 'take a seat', if you are interviewing them or if they are a guest who has come for dinner. There might even be ritual symbolism involved—the vicar at your church might ask you to 'sit or kneel to pray'.

Notice that in these examples, the one who has authority invites the other to sit. This is one of the reasons why it is important that Aslan leads the children to their thrones in *The Lion, The Witch and The Wardrobe*. It is also one of the reasons that James and John's request to Jesus is so surprising. They simply tell Jesus that they want to be seated beside him in heaven. They do not wait for Jesus to invite them to sit.

Even as I write this in a local coffee shop, an exchange of this kind happens. A student enters and awkwardly approaches the table where his professor sits. 'Is anyone sitting here? I mean, can I sit here?' He looks sheepish for having asked. The teacher follows the social custom and repeats the phrase in full, 'Please, take a seat.' Order is restored. Embedded in our language is the assumption that it is the one with the authority in the situation who offers the seat.

When James and John ask Jesus to give them whatever they desire, and proceed to request a seat by his side, they are seizing the initiative and the superiority. What's surprising about Jesus' response is that he does not chastise them for usurping his authority. He is, after all, the king of heaven and earth, so it would seem excusable for him to do so.

Instead, he claims that the details of the seating plan are being taken care of by someone even higher: 'to sit at my right hand or at my left is not mine to grant' (Mark 10:40). These seats, Jesus tells them, are 'for those for whom it has been prepared *by my Father*' (Matthew 20:23, my italics). A king of humility, he points constantly to the Father. If it is not for Jesus to declare who shall be seated where, it is certainly not for James and John, nor for us. This is why the book of James urges us so strongly not to show favouritism within the church when ushering people into the pews:

> Pause for a moment to think about the ways in which we speak about sitting down

'My brothers and sisters, believers in our glorious Lord Jesus Christ, don't show favouritism. Suppose a man comes into your meeting wearing a gold ring and fine clothes, and a poor man in shabby clothes also comes in. If you show special attention to the man wearing fine clothes and say, "Here's a good seat for you," but say to the poor man, "You stand there" or "Sit on the floor by my feet," have you not discriminated among yourselves and become judges with evil thoughts?' (James 2:1–4, NIV).

... loaded with significance

Where we sit is loaded with significance. It shapes our experience and it is noticed by God. However, we must always remember that wherever we are positioned in this life and in the life to come, we are part of a kingdom of humility. We must wait for God's lead, allowing him the authority to direct our movements. For, as Revelation makes clear, even those seated on thrones in the life to come will be in awe of Jesus: 'The seventh angel sounded his trumpet, and there were loud voices in heaven, saying: "The kingdom of the world has become the kingdom of our Lord and of his Messiah, and he will reign for ever and ever." And the twenty-four elders who sit on their thrones before God fell on their faces and worshipped God' (Revelation 11:15–16, NRSV).

It's the same message that Jesus shared with his disciples after they became disgruntled with James and John because of their ambitious desire. Our humility with regard to position is in contrast to the world around us: 'Jesus called them together and said, "You know that those who are regarded as rulers of the Gentiles lord it over them, and their high officials exercise authority over them. Not so with you. Instead, whoever wants to become great among you must be your servant, and whoever wants to be first must be slave of all. For even the Son of Man did not come to be served, but to serve, and to give his life as a ransom for many' (Mark 10:42–45, NIV).

In this way we are stationed as pointers to Jesus, the king who died for us and rose again. It's a truth that we celebrate each Easter, just as Helen described, with processions, candles, eggs... and maybe this year, with a well-deserved sit-down. In amid the business of this spring, it's important that we recognise the authority of Jesus as our servant-king, and take heed of his call to all of his disciples:

'Come away to a deserted place all by yourselves and rest a while' (Mark 6:31, NRSV).

My Space

This space is for you to make your own notes.

A place to pause on the journey, look at the view and anticipate the next step

GORDON GILES

Singing with the seated soul

Thou hast heard their reproach, O Lord, and all their imaginations against me; The lips of those that rose up against me, and their device against me all the day. Behold their sitting down, and their rising up; I am their musick.
LAMENTATIONS 3:61–63 (KJV)

author

Gordon Giles is Vicar of St Mary Magdalene, Enfield, and Director of Post-Ordination Training for the Edmonton Episcopal Area of London Diocese. He is the author of several books.

Do you sit comfortably when praying, when worshipping? Most of us try to sit comfortably when watching television, when talking to friends, when eating a meal or for almost any inactive leisure activity. We sit at the theatre and concerts; we sit in church. And when we are in church, we tend to sit for the readings and sermon, and if the choir or music group performs something, we sit for that. When we have gone to receive Communion, we will often sit and wait quietly while others go up to the rail. We might sit—or we might kneel—for the prayers. In a more formal choral evensong service, we would sit for the Psalm, readings and anthem but stand for the Magnificat and Nunc Dimittis, and we would be expected to kneel for the prayers.

Prayer is generally associated with kneeling—a posture of supplication and humility: a difficult, even painful posture for some. Singing is invariably done standing up—for good reason, as singing involves the inhalation and expulsion of air using the diaphragm, which is easier, more comfortable, powerful and effective when standing. Traditions of saying the Psalms hark back to singing plainsong in a gentle and reflective manner. Unlike robust hymn singing, this reflective, *listening* way of singing—or saying—the psalms requires a quietness and thinness of timbre, and sitting restricts the volume. If you can't hear the person next to you, you are making too much noise yourself. There is also a real sense that we are not speaking or singing *to* God, but are actually *listening* to God. And worship, while it is certainly about praise, is also, and perhaps more significantly, about listening to God, who speaks to us even as we sing to him.

In the medieval period, there were no chairs in churches; folk milled about, came and went, perhaps to catch the music, which largely went on while the priest celebrated Communion almost out of sight. Most of the people in the building would not actually receive Communion. But they might recognise some of the music, which they would hear standing up, even walking about. The architecture of medieval churches therefore made no provision for pews or chairs; at best there were stone benches set into the outer walls. Only those who could not stand used them, and thus it was said that 'the weakest went to the

Prayer is generally associated with kneeling—a posture of supplication and humility: a difficult, even painful posture for some

wall'. This began to change during the Reformation, as it brought with it an increased emphasis on the word, rather than the sacrament, which in turn made the sermon more important. Benches began to appear, and it became increasingly necessary to sit near the front in order to hear the sermon, and your pew was determined by your social standing and wealth. Pew rents were introduced, a practice which has not completely died out. Many a village church has box pews with a slot on the door for the name card of the 'owner', and woe betide the newcomer or visitor who sits in the wrong pew!

So, just as our posture for worship has a history and a meaning, so does our posture for **listening to music**

Customary to stand...

Although the Reformation had an impact on church music, in England particularly, such that as the congregation found themselves seated for worship (and were expected to be seen in the pews they rented), the amount of music used in churches diminished considerably. It was not until 1861 that the first widespread hymn book, *Hymns Ancient and Modern*, was published, and hymn-singing in churches is really only a phenomenon of the last century and a half. For physiological reasons, it is customary to stand to do so.

This slightly confusing history of posture and music serves as background to the almost universal modern practice of listening to music seated, on a concert hall chair, a hard wooden pew (cushions please!), or in an armchair at home. Where do you listen to music? Most people now listen to music in the car, on a train, at a concert, in church, or at home—all of which involve being seated. Music can be heard almost everywhere now; it is ubiquitous, in supermarkets, shops, restaurants and cafés, and iPods and their ilk can be used anywhere.

So, just as our posture for worship has a history and a meaning, so does our posture for listening to music. The posture we adopt reveals what we expect it to do for and to us. Walking about during worship implies a certain lack of attention and, to be fair, the priests at medieval masses were not particularly concerned with the involvement of the laity, who were not encouraged to receive the sacrament anyway: they were considered far too unworthy, and only the priest received. Similarly with music: if you walk about with an iPod, or have music on while chopping the vegetables or even driving the car, there is a sense in which you are not listening at all. The music—or the worship—goes in one ear and out the other. Some of the tasks we accompany with music do require significant concentration, and that means there is less attention (if any) truly to devote to the music. We might be *hearing* it, but there is a difference between hearing something and listening to it. *Listening* requires attention, exclusive attention, and you cannot give it that without sitting down and doing nothing else.

Few of us do this often at all. To sit and listen to a piece of music demands a certain discipline, an ability to avoid distraction, and of course it takes *time*. Music is the art of time, and there are no shortcuts: if a song is five minutes long, it takes five minutes to listen to it. There is, in fact, only one guaranteed way truly to pay attention to a piece of music, whether it is two minutes or two hours long, and that is to get hold of the score (the 'music', notated on paper) and follow it while listening. Not everyone has easy access to a score, for sure, but libraries and the internet make this significantly easier than it used to be. Another way is to play it oneself (but again, not an option for everyone!) *Listening* to music—as opposed to hearing it—is not actually that easy and requires some effort and determination.

To sit and listen to a piece of music demands a certain discipline, an ability to avoid distraction

Where music is accompanied by words, it is easier, because the text—if

For many people, sitting quietly with music playing is a form of **spiritual exercise**

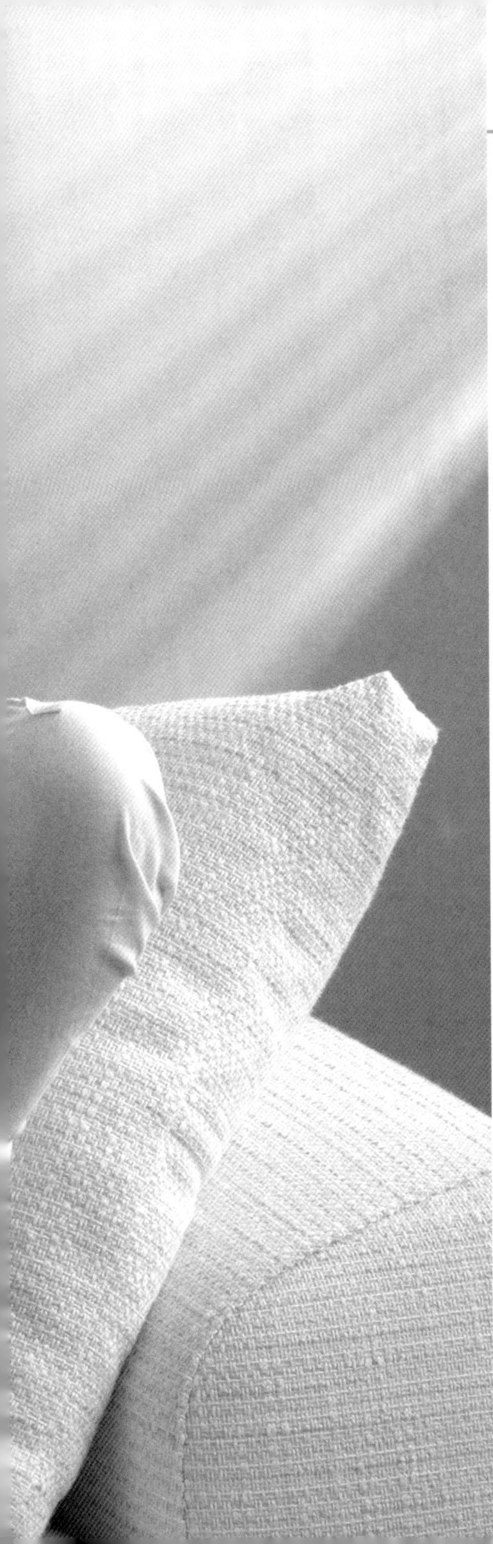

it can be understood—makes for a very good guide rope on the journey through the music. Thus a piece of choral or vocal music can have a story to tell, and if it is a biblical text, it may already be familiar. But even in doing this, you still need to sit down and avoid distraction. While music can be treated very badly indeed, and is an uncomplaining victim of mistreatment, it will reward devotion and attention in ways that can achieve nothing short of *change* in its listeners. Music can change us by taking us on a journey, such that when we arrive at the conclusion of a great symphony or opera or oratorio, we may have travelled a great distance emotionally or spiritually. And it can all be done in First Class seats.

In this, music and personal spiritually go hand in hand. For many people, sitting quietly with music playing is a form of spiritual exercise, or 'chill-out' time. For some this has a divine dimension, while others will talk only in terms of relaxation. There are three things that need be said about this:

Firstly, there is a danger that 'chilling out' to music is assumed to be prayerful. It might be, but it can certainly not be. Listening to music—even to deeply sacred music—is not an excuse for or a substitute for prayer. Lighting a candle and putting Fauré's *Requiem* on the hi-fi and relaxing in a comfy chair is not a substitute for prayer, and while it may create an atmosphere which feels prayerful, the listening and speaking to God that prayer entails and involves must always be distinguished from the music itself. Music can be prayer, of course, but in order for it to be more than the prayer of the composer or performer, we must make it our own, and that means paying attention both to the music and to God. As we have already seen, that is not easy: paying attention to music is hard, and paying attention to God is hard; doing both together could be doubly difficult.

... there are techniques and approaches which can make a musical spirituality possible

Yet all is not lost, for there are techniques and approaches which can make a musical spirituality possible and powerful. The other two points I want to make concern a weak and a strong form of music with prayer.

Thus, secondly, it is worth acknowledging that for some, the ability to hear—rather than listen to—music can be a gift. For while it may be true that if you listen to music while doing something else, you are not completely *listening* to it, many people find it to be very useful in order to avoid distraction. Music can filter out distractions while being a pleasant background in itself. Music creates mood, and can help us concentrate on something else. This is why supermarkets play music, and the Musak Corporation was created specifically to produce a particular kind of non descript music which would enable workers to be more productive, not distracted and subliminally encouraged in their tasks. There is no doubt as to the success of this phenomenon. This is not to denigrate the approach: it is very effective, and can be very useful in one's prayer life. If you are the kind of person for whom music of an appropriate mood enables you to focus on the job in hand, and your desire is to meet God, then, whether you are sitting quietly at home or meditating during the anthem at choral evensong, you can find a still place of divine encounter within a cocoon of beautiful sound.

There is another, third point, which draws on what I have already said. For rather than *hearing* music as a means to prayer, it is also possible truly to *listen* to it and thereby to gain spiritual insights from the passing of musical time. Turn down the lights, light the candle, sit in a comfy chair and put on the music, as above. However, do not let the music wash over you, but rather pray through attentive listening. If it is Fauré's *Requiem,* for example, get a vocal score or the text and follow it word for word, note for note. Marvel at what the composer does and at the meaning of the words. *Notice* the pleas for mercy, the assurance of forgiveness, the inner peace of resurrection life painted and sounded in the music. Make them your own, as if it is *your* song: sing with your soul, such that as the final chords fade away you have personally been on the music's journey of plea and praise. God is in the music, but you have to seek him, and that means paying attention—truly *listening* and just as Jesus calls us to 'come, follow me' in life, so too do we need to follow the music in order to find him in the path the words and notes take. Not only is this approach an effective way to sit and listen to music prayerfully, it is, of course, a metaphor for all our encounters with God. It is easy to wander through life with God in the background, a constant companion perhaps, but one to whom we never actually listen: a companion with whom we rarely, if ever, sit down to talk and listen to—someone with whom we rarely actually have a *conversation*. Music can broker such a conversation, and in that much, as in so many other ways, it truly is a gift for which to sit down and give thanks.

Prayer

God of sound and silence, whose voice brought forth creation yet stilled the waves, hear our prayers and speak to us in the beauty of music, that the melody of your love song may be united with the chords of our praise, that in harmony together we may walk in the way of Christ on earth and in heaven. Amen

TONY HORSFALL

Learning to sit

author

Tony Horsfall is a freelance trainer and retreat leader, living in Yorkshire. He has written a number of books, including *Working from a Place of Rest* (BRF, 2010) and *Mentoring for Spiritual Growth* (BRF, 2008), and contributes to *New Daylight* Bible reading notes. For further information, see www.brfonline.org.uk.

Watchman Nee (1903–72) was one of China's greatest Christian leaders, controversial to some, but widely respected for his whole-hearted devotion to God and his ability as a Bible teacher. He was given the rather unusual name 'Watchman' because it was his mother's prayer that he would be one who would warn others of danger or arouse them to opportunity.

Nee was a third-generation Christian, converted as an 18-year-old student through the preaching of the itinerant evangelist Dora Yu. At once he saw the implications of his decision to follow Christ, recognising that it meant a life-long obedience to one whose demands were justifiably total.

Shortly after his conversion, he left home to spend a year studying the

His early 20s were a time for proving the faithfulness of God in various ways and for **growing in faith**

Bible under the guidance of Miss Yu. His love of the scriptures, and his profound insight into their meaning, characterised his whole life. He returned to his home in Foochow to finish his college studies and, finding a few other young men of faith, quickly formed an evangelistic band to reach out to other students with great effect.

An Anglican missionary, Margaret Barber, took him under her wing and became a mentor to him. He was both zealous and headstrong as a young man, and it took some straight talking from her to keep him on the right path. He had a great appetite for learning and devoured her library of Christian writings. In particular, he wanted to understand the cross. Already he had begun home meetings on Sundays where his followers could break bread together and worship God in this informal setting.

His early 20s were a time for proving the faithfulness of God in various ways and for growing in faith. He believed that if God sends you, he will support you, and lived by the principle 'give, and it will be given to you' (Luke 6:38, NIV). Time and again he saw God provide for him financially. Having decided to give himself fully to the work of the gospel, he began a series of preaching tours and learned to

It meant a lifelong obedience to one whose demands were justifiably total

trust God to demonstrate his power to unbelieving hearers of the message.

Not everything went smoothly for him. Some of his friends took exception

Although later they acknowledged they had made a mistake, this wounded Nee deeply, causing him to reflect on his ways. He began to realise that the preacher matters to God as much as the preaching…

to his preaching style and perhaps to his independence from the more traditional churches and asked him to stop attending their house meetings. Although later they acknowledged they had made a mistake, this wounded Nee deeply, causing him to reflect on his ways. He began to realise that the preacher matters to God as much as the preaching, and that God would need to work out in him what he would proclaim through him.

Opportunity came for him to visit Malaya for a preaching trip, providing further opportunity to develop his understanding of the gospel. From his early days he had produced a magazine called *Revival*, and this provided a platform for him to share with others his ideas and reflections. By his mid-20s his unique approach to the gospel was taking shape.

Part of Nee's effectiveness as a preacher lay in his ability to make plain that the way to God lies solely through the finished work of Christ. All too many Christians in China were prone to strive after a salvation based on their own good works, an approach little removed from the Buddhism in which they had grown up. In his teaching on Ephesians (published in 1952 as *Sit, Walk, Stand*) he sought to help his hearers grasp the point that Christianity does not begin with a big DO but with a big DONE.

Here was a great truth that he had grasped in his own early years as a believer—that the Christian life from start to finish is based upon the principle of utter dependence on Jesus. Having died on the cross for our sins, he sat down at the right hand of God

> Here was a great truth that he had grasped in his own early years as a believer…

(Hebrews 1:3; Ephesians 1:20), having completed the work of salvation. We are now invited to sit with him (Ephesians 2:6) and to share in the benefits of his finished work.

But what does it mean to 'sit down'? It means that by faith we are to cease from striving to make ourselves right with God and instead to rest in what he has done for us at the cross. We are simply to step by faith into the enjoyment of all he has provided for us. 'It is not that we work for God,' Nee says, 'but that He works for us. God gives us our position of rest. He brings his finished work and presents it to us, and then He says, "Please sit" (*ch'eng tso*)' (*Sit, Walk, Stand*).

For Nee, the whole of our Christian experience continues on this basis of not depending on our own work but always relying on the prior work of God. Every new spiritual experience begins with a new 'sitting down'. We can receive the Spirit because of the exaltation of Jesus, and the outpouring of the Spirit at Pentecost (Acts 2:33). We are 'in Christ' and united with him because of God's direct action (1 Corinthians 1:30). We can be free from sin because we have been crucified with Christ (Galatians 2:20).

These are great historic facts, and we enter into them by faith. The Christian life begins with our sitting down.

For Reflection

As far as Nee is concerned, we have to sit before we can walk. What do you think he means by this?

Why does he say Christianity begins with a big DONE rather than a big DO?

Would you say you have learned to 'sit down' in this way as yet? If not, what prevents you?

Margaret's Space

Margaret Harvey is a retired priest in the Church in Wales. She has been running Coleg y Groes Retreat House. Margaret writes a regular column in *Quiet Spaces*.

'Sit'—some ideas for meditating

That's what you say to the dog. 'Si**t**'. Firmly. With the stress on the '**t**'. To say it like that to another human being smacks of arrogance, dominance and rudeness. So we usually seem to add another, qualifying word.

'Sit down'

I think back to childhood and the beginning of the school day. As the teacher walked into the classroom, we were expected to stand (I don't know if this still happens today!) until the teacher told us to 'sit down'. So much would depend on the tone of voice and the expression on the face. A sharpness of tone would put us in our places. The teacher remained standing, asserting authority, while we were the inferiors—children expected to be seen rather than heard. Or the facial expression might show that the teacher had a lot on her mind and the tone of voice reflected that. The command felt quite impersonal. As a class we were to sit down and keep quiet and cause no trouble. Sometimes 'sit down' would be said with exasperation. 'For goodness' sake, sit down so that we can get on with things.' If all was well, however, 'sit down' had an air of anticipation about

Love bade me welcome; yet my soul drew back,
Guilty of dust and sin.
But quick-eyed Love, observing me grow slack
From my first entrance in,
Drew nearer to me, sweetly questioning
If I lack'd anything.

'A guest,' I answer'd, 'worthy to be here':
Love said, 'You shall be he.'
'I, the unkind, ungrateful? Ah, my dear,
I cannot look on Thee.'
Love took my hand and smiling did reply,
'Who made the eyes but I?'

'Truth, Lord; but I have marr'd them: let my shame
Go where it doth deserve.'
'And know you not,' says Love, 'who bore the blame?'
'My dear, then I will serve.'
'You must sit down,' says Love, 'and taste my meat.'
So I did sit and eat.

GEORGE HERBERT (1593–1633)

it. The day was about to begin. The teacher sat down too. Together we were about to begin something. The tone of voice can change everything.

Read the story of the feeding of the five thousand in John 6:1–15. Jesus tells his disciples, 'Have the people sit down' (v. 10, NIV). The crowd sits on the green grass. Let your imagination walk around in the story. Imagine being in one of the clumps of people, chatting together, looking, having a day out, discussing what you've heard and seen, and holding out your hands for food as the friends of Jesus get to your group. This is sitting down in order to receive.

> Discovering where and how we can serve God and one another is **vitally important**

John's account of the feeding of the five thousand states that Jesus sat down with his disciples (v. 3). He is together with them, not standing over them. No wonder the writer is so amazed. This is Emmanuel; God with us; God sitting down with us; God inviting us to sit down with him, whoever we are.

Sometimes it is difficult to receive. 'What do you do?' we tend to ask new acquaintances. New members in a small church are looked at speculatively. Which vacant job can they fill? Discovering where and how we can serve God and one another is vitally important. But equally important, in the words of George Herbert (see the poem on page 43), is that 'you must sit down' and receive.

Luke describes Mary doing just this in Luke 10:38–42. In that busy household it was misunderstood and criticised. Sitting down to receive rather than doing can feel like a selfish waste of time. The vital importance of this kind of praying—sometimes called 'contemplative prayer'—is being rediscovered. (For further exploration try 'Contemplative Fire' www.contemplativefire.org and the Worth Abbey website www.worthabbey.net).

'Sit up'

Once we had sat down, the teacher would then tell us to 'sit up'! 'Sit up' meant 'pay attention'. It is about being attentive, keeping alert, keeping awake. When Jesus said to his disciples at Gethsemane, 'Sit here while I pray' (Mark 14:32) he wanted them to keep alert and watching rather than going to sleep. Sometimes prayer can be just that—sitting with Jesus, attentively, being present while he prays.

In our noisy and active culture we need to practise listening in order to help us to be attentive to God's small and quiet voice. Try taking a few minutes simply to listen to whatever sounds are around with complete attention. If you find it difficult to find a place that is silent, allow the sounds to be an aid for attentiveness rather than a distraction. How many sounds can you hear? Is there anything you have not noticed before? Focus on each sound in turn and allow it to turn into prayer and praise—for yourself as you listen to your breathing or heartbeat; for the people you can hear next door or in the street, on the road or in the air; for the creation around you.

The instruction to 'sit up' is also a very practical one about posture. It is of course possible to pray anywhere and in any way. However, just as it is easier to get to sleep if we arrange our body suitably, usually lying down, so the posture of our body can help attentiveness in prayer. It is helpful, especially if we are aiming to pray for any length of time, to sit with a straight back and with the feet on the ground.

'Sit still'

Sitting still is perhaps the most difficult thing to do, for adults as well as for children. We want to be up and doing, to influence events, to be in control. In the story of the exodus in the Old Testament, the Israelites again and again had to struggle with impatience. Waiting for God is often the hardest thing to do. We so much want events to unfold quickly, solutions to arrive immediately, problems to be solved without our having to wait around. Try reading the book of Exodus with this in mind. Chapter 14 is a good example. 'The Lord will fight for you; you need only to be **still**' (Exodus 14:14), Moses tells the anxious people.

We need to practise listening in order to help us to be attentive to God's small and quiet voice

Practise being still. Find a smooth pebble and use it as a way into stillness. Take some time to feel the smoothness of the stone. Look at its colour and texture. Feel its weight in your hand. Appreciate the time that has gone into the forming of the stone. Great forces have gone into its making. Now it is small and still. Hold it as you pray.

My Space

This space is for you to make your own notes.

A place to pause on the journey, look at the view and anticipate the next step

© *sunsetman / Shutterstock.com*

LIZ PACEY

Prayers

To prepare for prayer find a place where you can sit quietly. Perhaps light a candle as a sign of God's presence and have your Bible open beside you

Light a candle as a sign

to show you are ready to receive his word. Pause for a moment to reflect on what sitting means to you: an almost unheard-of luxury, a welcome break, a necessity, a waste of time? Is it passive or active? We focus now on what sitting might mean to us and to others.

author

Liz Pacey is a Reader in the Church of England, a freelance writer and a mature theology and ministry student.

You will keep in perfect peace those whose minds are steadfast, because they trust in you.
ISAIAH 26:3 (TNIV)

Prayer

Lord, already I feel your peace washing over me. I know this is only a temporary respite from all the cares that seek to engulf me but I so need this time with you. I know I'll go out into my world and yours better able to cope with all that comes my way. But do I really expect you to speak to me right now?

Pause for a moment to reflect on what sitting means to you...

The Lord appeared to Abraham near the great trees of Mamre while he was sitting at the entrance to his tent in the heat of the day.
GENESIS 18:1

Prayer

There are so many places where we might choose to sit. By the sea on a beautiful day. In an empty church or a full church. Over a cup of tea with friends or a candlelit dinner with someone special. In your mind's eye choose a lovely place and allow Jesus to join you there.

Lord, you sometimes come to us unexpectedly. May we be like Abraham, ready and eager to respond.

❖

As Jesus approached Jericho, a blind man was sitting by the roadside begging.
LUKE 18:35

Prayer

Then there are some places where we would avoid sitting if we could. The dentist's or hospital waiting room. In an exam or a hospital bed. Allow Jesus to join you somewhere you really do not want to be. How do you feel about sitting there now?

One of those days Jesus went out to a mountainside to pray, and spent the night praying to God.
LUKE 6:12

Prayer

Night can be a lonely time, particularly if we're watching over an ill person or just can't sleep because of our problems.

Lord, please come to those who watch or are alone at night.

❖

After three days they found him in the temple courts, sitting among the teachers, listening to them and asking them questions.
LUKE 2:46

Prayer

Lord, what a lovely picture this is of you sitting in your Father's house. You're using the time wisely, not only drinking in knowledge but questioning too. You wanted so much to learn. Lord, help me to sit quietly in your presence, wherever I am, hearing what you have to say to me, not being frightened to ask you questions. You don't want me to have a blind faith but to try to understand all you have to teach me. Help me to learn patiently, Lord.

I wait for you to
speak to me...

© Blend Images / Shutterstock.com

As Jesus and his disciples were on their way, he came to a village where a woman named Martha opened her home to him. She had a sister called Mary, who sat at the Lord's feet listening to what he said.
LUKE 10:38–39

Prayer

Lord, I've read the story of Martha and Mary many times, and there is always this tension over whether it's better to sit or to be on the go. Help me to realise that there is room for both action and repose in my life and that I need to seek and find balance. Grant me the opportunity to sit alongside you with the people I love. And if they don't love you yet, let there be nothing about me that will prevent them coming to you.

Enjoying conversations
with passing strangers...

Jesus said, 'Have the people sit down.' There was plenty of grass in that place, and they sat down (about five thousand men were there).
JOHN 6:10

Prayer

I used to love sitting on the floor but now, Lord, as I'm getting older, my joints aren't really up to it. When people commented, I used to joke 'I know my place.' Actually, what better place could there be than sitting on the floor at Jesus' feet?

I close my eyes now and imagine just that. The room is filled with his presence—it's hard to explain, but it's somehow majestic and friendly and compassionate at the same time. How I need this time with you, Lord! I wait for you to speak to me. Forgive me, Lord, for not doing this more often.

❖

Therefore go and make disciples of all nations...
MATTHEW 28:19

Prayer

Thank you Lord, for the privilege of being an armchair traveller. I don't have to move at all from my chair, yet through newspapers, television, radio, I can travel the world. And the really brilliant thing is that I can take you with me. Thank you, Lord, for the opportunity to take an informed interest in your world and to be able to pray for those who most need it.

❖

Peace I leave with you; my peace I give you. I do not give to you as the world gives. Do not let your hearts be troubled and do not be afraid.
JOHN 14:27

Meditation

Sitting can be done in many different ways and can tell many stories. Be aware of others as they sit, of what their body language tells you about their needs.

Go on a bus journey and notice how people sit there. On edge, watching for their stop. Uncomfortably under a load of shopping. Keeping a watchful eye on their offspring. Frowning with the cares of the world. Smiling happily. Very publicly chatting on their mobile phones or to their companions, not caring who hears. Enjoying conversations with passing strangers before perhaps going home to empty houses. Thank God for the glimpses into these different worlds and spend your sitting time praying for them.

HEATHER FENTON

Sitting under the great oaks of Mamre

'I'll unload the shopping when I have had a couple of minutes sitting down,' I find myself saying yet again. Sometimes I find that the half-hour journey to the supermarket, buying the things and coming back can be very tiring, although I never used to feel like this! So it seems that as we get older we tend to think about sitting down more often.

author

Heather Fenton works as a parish priest and an editor.

If you realise that this is happening to you or to someone you know, you may find it rather discouraging. So did I, until I was reading Abram's story in Genesis. If you look at this, you will see that his initial call happened when he was 75 years old, when he heard God's call and responded. At a time when he might be expected to have a very strong commitment to going on living where he had been for years, he had to give up that familiar, presumably reassuring place, full of family memories. This was not downsizing now the family had grown up; he had to take his family 'and all the possessions they had accumulated and all the people they

He had to give up that familiar, presumably reassuring place, full of family memories. This was not downsizing...

Time for a rest...

had acquired in Haran' (Genesis 12:5, NIV).

At about this point, my boot-full of groceries for the next fortnight slipped gently into perspective. Yes, I had seen a couple of people I knew while shopping (that is the way of things when you live somewhere quite remote) but had definitely not 'acquired' any people. I climbed into my comfortable car and headed home. Abram climbs on to his rather less comfortable transport and heads off, God knows where!

God knows that Abram needs encouragement and a sense that he is getting this strange plan right. God confirms part of his special plan to Abram by appearing to him by 'the great tree of Moreh at Shechem' and telling him that 'to your offspring I will give this land' (vv. 6–7). Abram, for all his 75 years, has to travel on because the time for the fulfilment of this promise lies in the future, and in travelling he has all sorts of adventures and challenges. So 'retirement', that strange modern idea that at a certain age we can opt out and please ourselves, is not on the cards. Instead, he has to face many new challenges, giving him plenty of opportunities for sitting or walking or standing, not least because he would want time to think, to wonder, to pray.

Abram, as he is still called, has to pass through some difficult situations. You can read about some of these: for example, his trip to Egypt, caused by a famine (12:14–20); a personal economic boom (13:1–2); facing some environmental issues (vv. 5–6) and some family problems (13:7–14:16). It all sounds a bit too familiar! Those of us who are among the 'post-war baby boomers' and who are currently fashionable as the focus of criticism in the media (regarding wealthy older people thoughtlessly causing problems and leaving a legacy of poor environmental policies) may recognise some of these in this light too. Through it all, Abram receives help and encouragement from God. The most fascinating to my mind is the amazing encounter with Melchizedek, a priest who can be seen as a type of Christ (14:18–20; see also Hebrews 7:1–17).

Other things happen in this story and by the time we get to Genesis 17, we discover that Abram is 90 years old, so another 15 years have passed! Surely poor Abram can rightly claim it is now time for a rest. But no, it is time for a new name, Abraham (Genesis 17:5). This comes together with confirmation of God's covenant and, rather startlingly for an elderly childless couple, reference to many descendants. At this point Abraham, who seems to have been pretty good at trusting God so far, decides this is a good idea but it needs putting into practice by him. Unfortunately, in doing this he sets up a dysfunctional aspect to family life—something else which could resonate with those of us who are of the baby boomer generation.

> God knows that Abram needs encouragement and a sense that he is getting this strange plan right

The oaks of Mamre seem to be a favourite location for this nomadic family. They have already been mentioned as a camp site a number of times (13:18; 14:13) and in chapter 18 we find Abraham, as he now is, there yet again. And yes, he is sitting there and is probably tired too—travelling, for someone who is 99 years old, is wearisome! It is in the heat of the day, so time for a rest. Suddenly Abraham looks up and sees three men standing nearby. In line with cultural expectations, he hurries to greet them and offers them a little water for washing and a resting place (18:3–4). Finding Sarah, his wife, he asks her to cook up a quick meal (vv. 5–6). (Well, not so very quick as it turns out—the meal is still grazing nearby!)

Sarah is probably hot and tired. She is elderly and her afternoon nap has been disturbed. Her husband has invited

The picture of oaks of Mamre reproduced above can be found here: http://en.wikipedia.org/wiki/File:Tristram383.jpg
There are quite a lot of icons showing this story and a selection of them can be found at www.icon-art.info/topic.php?lng=en&top_id=204
Ann Persson has recently written The Circle of Love *(BRF, 2010), which helps us to consider the most famous of these icons,* The Holy Trinity. *A copy of the icon appears on the front cover of the book and may be found at http://en.wikipedia.org/wiki/Holy_Trinity_Icon*

the visitors to stay and he doesn't just want a quick stew, he wants some bread, and curds and milk too (v. 6). From inside the tent, she can hear Abraham talking to the guests. What is it that they are saying to him? The writer of Genesis identifies the speaker as 'the Lord', whom Sarah hears telling Abraham that he will 'surely return to you about this time next year, and Sarah your wife will have a son' (v. 10). Sarah is old; Sarah is tired; Sarah thinks she is being realistic. 'Me! No way!' she thinks and laughs to herself. The Lord, who hears the secrets of hearts, rather politely points out to Abraham that Sarah has just laughed (v. 13). Abraham, like every good husband, probably knows that is exactly what Sarah would do if she had heard. Nothing turns out to be too hard for the Lord, who can 'hear' what we are thinking; he is so much closer than even the closest of husbands! Sarah is afraid, so tries to get out of it by telling a lie.

Later the men get up to leave but warn Abraham and Sarah of the disaster about to hit Sodom and Gomorrah, and so the story of God's leading for this little family goes on. God enables them to become the ancestors of a very great nation indeed.

And it all happened to an elderly couple. An elderly couple who probably

The Holy Trinity by Andrei Rublev

wanted to stay at home, who got tired, and hot, and overstretched on a hot day. Yes, God used older people to fulfil his intentions for the world! 'Is anything too hard for the Lord?' (v. 14).

So take a seat. Yes, put your feet up and think about it. Too old? Never! And please note, Abraham died when he was 175—'a good old age, an old man and full of years' (25:8).

CAROL JERMAN

Tides and Seasons:

Modern prayers in the Celtic tradition

David Adam, SPCK, reissued 2010

David Adam's book *Tides and Seasons: Modern prayers in the Celtic tradition* has been written not as a take-it-or-leave-it set of prayers but as an exhortation to discover the presence and wisdom of God in every ebb and flow of our lives. Like many others, David Adam sees in the Celtic tradition an antidote to our increasingly fragmented lives, and so has written this essentially practical book, encouraging us to experience the interrelatedness of all things, held together in the love of God.

author

Carol Jerman is a Reader in the Church in Wales.

The prayers are presented as simple poems, very accessible and easy to understand, but never trite. There are quiet proclamations of trust in the love of

... an exhortation to discover the presence and wisdom of God **in every ebb and flow of our lives**

Christ and prayers to lift the heart to the triune Creator God. There are prayers of rejoicing as part of a whole worshipping creation and prayers that acknowledge the immanence of God in all things, in all the changing tides of our experience.

There are also three types of prayer particular to Celtic tradition, the *caim*, the *rune* and the *lorica*. The book falls into four sections, 'Incoming Tide', 'Full Tide', 'Ebb Tide' and 'Low Tide', and each section has its own introduction and conclusion. The introductions consider the particular challenges and blessings of that stage of the tide and the conclusions are both devotional and instructive. David Adam's experience as

a spiritual director is evident. To me, the real strength of this refreshing book lies in these prose passages that surround the prayers. This is material for personal devotions, asking us to take the time to be still and meditative. Many of the poems are also very suitable for use in public ministry. The Revd Canon David Adam was Vicar of the Holy Island of Lindisfarne for 13 years, and his observation of the changing tide as a picture of our lives rings true.

Great High Priest

Christ great High Priest,
Risen on high,
Christ offering life
Never to die.

Christ great High Priest,
Ascended above,
Come down O Lord
Cover with love.

Christ great High Priest,
Back from the dead,
Show us your Presence
In the Bread.

Christ great High Priest,
Saviour Divine
Give us yourself
In the red Wine.

My Space

This space is for you to make your own notes.

A place to pause on the journey, look at the view and anticipate the next step

© sunsetman / Shutterstock.com

HEATHER FENTON

Sitting together

... find a tree. Sit and look at it, either from afar or close up...

Elsewhere in this issue I have written an article about older people, namely Abraham and Sarah, sitting under the oaks of Mamre. I guess they grew to know those trees pretty well. You may like to take a small group for a walk in order to look at, or even sit under, a suitable tree. Or you could do this all by yourself.

We may not have any ancient oaks to sit under, as they did, but most people can find a tree or two at which to look. Even if you live in a city, do not despair! Recently I was in London and walked past a number of those plane trees, otherwise known as *Platanus x acerifolia*, which I think are quite magnificent. Stopping to look properly at one of them, I looked in detail at this tree's strong single trunk, maybe between 20 and 35 metres high—so very tall! I am always fascinated by bark because there are such lovely textures and this was no exception. I saw that this bark often flakes off in

author

Heather Fenton works as a parish priest and an editor.

patches, leaving a dappled look. The leaves vary in shape, even on the same tree, and the colour is from medium to dark green and may be slightly yellow on a younger tree. They may be glossy or matt. Most fascinating of all are the fruits, which are spherical and hang downwards in groups like small brown balls on the end of a short string. Unfortunately too high to touch, they are well worth taking a proper look.

Anyway, find a tree. Sit and look at it, either from afar or close up, or even do both! Look at the overall shape of the tree first. Is it a single trunk or very branched? Does it look as if it has been there a long time, or is it small and struggling upwards to the light because there is too much competition around? You may like to try to describe it to one another if you are in a group. Now go up closer. What is the bark like? Rough or smooth? Patterned by colour or by texture—or both?

See the elaborate structure of the canopy. Admire the detail of what God has made

I am always fascinated by bark because there are such lovely textures

What shape are the leaves, and are they all the same? Can you see the structure of the leaf? How would you describe their colour? Is this tree a common one where you are now, or is it an exotic import from elsewhere?

Finally, sit under the tree if at all possible. Peer up into the branches. See the elaborate structure of the canopy. Admire the detail of what God has made.

After your walk you could spend some time of quiet together, recollecting what you have seen and touched and discussing God's gift of trees to us.

One day God will bring healing to the nations of the world, and there will be the tree of life...

Read quietly Isaiah 55:12. One day, he tells us, 'the trees of the field shall clap their hands' (NIV). At the moment the creation is subjected to frustration (Romans 8:20), but eventually 'the creation itself will be liberated from its bondage to decay and brought into the glorious freedom of the children of God' (v. 21).

One day God will bring healing to the nations of the world, and there will be the tree of life: 'the leaves of the tree are for the healing of the nations' (Revelation 22:2). The trees will indeed 'clap their hands' as they too are set free, together with all the people of God.

Prayer

Lord God, creator of all things, we thank you for trees. We thank you for their detail. We thank you for texture, shape, and colour. We thank you for the variety.

We remember with sadness that it was in taking of fruit from a forbidden tree that sin came into the world, but we remember with great gladness the salvation from sin that came because of the work of Christ on the tree of the cross.

Help us to live as those who expect to see the wholeness of the world restored. While we wait for that restoration, enable us to journey on through your world, noticing the beautiful things and living as those who will one day know ourselves to be fully part of your new creation. Amen

The Lord reigneth; let the people tremble: he sitteth between the cherubims; let the earth be moved.

PSALM 99:1 KJV

In the year that King Uzziah died, I saw the Lord, high and exalted, seated on a throne; and the train of his robe filled the temple.

ISAIAH 6:1 NIV

He who was seated on the throne said, 'I am making everything new!'

REVELATION 21:5A

JOHN BIRCH

Worthy are you

author

John Birch is a Methodist Lay Preacher and worship leader and lives in Wales. He contributes to the International Bible Reading Fellowship notes, and his prayers have appeared on various websites. You can find more material on his website www.faithandworship.com.

Worthy are you
Worthy are you
Lamb of God to receive from us
the worship and praise
that's due your name
As with the angels we proclaim
Worthy are you
Worthy are you
Lamb of God, slain for us
you shed your blood
to pay the price
of sinfulness through sacrifice
Now to Him who sits on the throne
and the Lamb who leads us home
Be Praise and Honour
and Glory and Power
for ever and ever
Amen

ANN PERSSON

Time for Reflection

This meditation is taken from *Time for Reflection: Meditations to use through the year*, a book of biblically rooted meditations, which aims to provide accessible and practical routes to exploring prayer as that way of being in God's presence, letting the sediment of our lives settle so that we may have a true reflection of ourselves and of God within us.

author

Ann Persson enjoys combining her love of nature and her love of God's word. She leads Quiet Days and has also written *The Circle of Love* (BRF, 2010). For further information, see www.brfonline.org.uk.

The tree of life

This is an exercise that will give you the opportunity to stop and take stock of your life as it is at present. It is a disciplined exercise and could take you up to four hours to tackle it in depth, so you will need to choose a time when you are not likely to be interrupted. It would be even better to go away for a day's retreat so that you are not surrounded by reminders of jobs to be done or a telephone to be answered.

You will need a large piece of paper

... hard to imagine our landscape without trees. They add so much to the beauty around us

(A3), some scrap paper, a pencil and a rubber. You may like to use some coloured crayons or felt pens.

You will be using the analogy of a tree with its roots, trunk and branches as a way of mapping out your life with its present commitments and relationships.

It would be hard to imagine our landscape without trees. They add so much to the beauty around us at every season of the year, whether dressed in lime at springtime, the green of summer, or dazzling autumn colours—or bereft of leaves but showing the tracery of bare branches etched against a winter sky. They offer shade from the heat and protection from the storm and accommodate a whole world of insects, squirrels and birds. For the most part, they outlive us, and when we plant a tree we plant for posterity. I saw some ancient oaks in the grounds of Blenheim Palace, Oxfordshire, which are about 600 years old and yet have life in them. One, which has the name King Harry, is 800 years old and still bears leaf.

I want to start with some facts about trees, to provide background for the exercise that follows.

The trunk of a broad-leaved tree divides at a certain height into a few thick, upward- or outward-growing branches that divide further and further to form the crown, which may be oval or round depending on the species. This shape provides the leaves with the greatest amount of light and air, ensuring the best conditions for the nourishment of the tree.

... the opportunity to stop and take stock of your life as it is at present

The tree is anchored in the ground by means of roots, which also serve to supply it with water and mineral

All the elements for growth are provided for the tree…

nutrients and act as storage for reserve food supplies. The roots take up the same area below ground as the branches do above.

All the elements for growth are provided for the tree: carbon dioxide in the air, radiant energy from the sun, rain water and the dissolved minerals it contains, and the nutrients from the soil in which the tree is planted. The tree obtains nourishment from the soil through the roots and from the air through the leaves, which are spread out as advantageously as possible. Like all flowering plants, trees bear fruit, reproduce and spread naturally by means of seed.

The way the tree grows is influenced by its environment—whether it grows in open ground with space around it or whether it grows in competition with other trees in a forest and has to reach high to find the sunlight.

The exercise

Before you begin, take some time to sit in quietness with God, your Creator and your loving father. Ask for the help of the Holy Spirit to give you insight and understanding.

Be prepared to draw a tree on your A3 paper. First, take a piece of scrap paper and jot down some answers to these questions, as you think about what kind of tree might represent you and about the conditions it might grow in.

- ❖ What species of tree will you choose—a broad, strong oak, a graceful birch, a tall beech or another?
- ❖ Is your tree wide and spreading (in which case you might need to turn your A3 paper horizontally) or is it tall and upright (so that you need to turn the paper vertically)?
- ❖ What is the season of the year in terms of your life experience?
- ❖ What is the prevailing weather in your life at the moment—for example, sunny and calm, stormy and challenging, cold and frosty?
- ❖ What would you describe as the soil conditions of your life—fertile, stony, damp or dry?

It does not matter whether you feel you can draw a tree or not, as your picture can be very basic and simple or as artistic as you want it to be. As you start to draw, consider the following:

- ❖ It is the roots that anchor and nourish you. Who or what does that for you? Draw the roots and label each one.
- ❖ Thinking of the trunk—what are your

strengths, and what do you feel your calling is to be or do? (I found it easier to name my trunk after I had thought about the branches and leaves: see the following points.)

- The main branches are the dominant areas of activity in your life. You may find that some of your branches echo your roots. For example, if your family is a strong root in your life, you will probably have a branch labelled 'family' too, as family business probably uses a fair amount of your time. The same could be said for church.

What are your strengths, and what do you feel your calling is to be or do?

- The smaller branches are the specific activities relating to the main branch. For example, if church is one of your main branches, smaller branches leading off would be the specific areas you are involved in, which could be youth work, playing a musical instrument in worship and being part of a weekly home group.
- The leaves are the jobs that are necessary for each small branch. To develop the main church branch further, the jobs would be those associated with each activity, so youth work could involve producing the publicity material, booking the hall, meeting with others to plan the programme and any other jobs that might occur to you.

You could also ask yourself:

- Are any branches damaged, dead or broken off and lying on the ground? These can represent commitments, people or jobs that are no longer playing an active part in your life but are still influential.
- Are there any scars of past wounds on your tree?
- Does your tree bear fruit?
- Is it offering shelter, rest or food for others?

This may sound an exhausting exercise to do in such detail but it is well worth it because, at the end, you will have a full picture of what is going on in your life. When you have finished your drawing and labelling, take a break and walk away from it for a short while.

For reflection

When you return, take a look at the finished result and write down any observations that come to you.

- ❖ Is there a branch for recreation?
- ❖ Which parts demand too much energy and drain you?
- ❖ Which areas give you energy and enjoyment, even though they may involve hard work? Which bits are downright unpleasant?
- ❖ Are there areas of duty that are getting squeezed because there is not really enough space for them?
- ❖ Do the chosen branches of activity reflect the words that you put on the trunk? In other words, are you doing and being what you feel called to do and be—or is there a mismatch?
- ❖ How do you feel about your tree?

Then, in your imagination, walk with God in the garden until you come upon your tree. Let him look at it and comment on it. Listen and then write down what you sense he may be saying. As a result of what you hear, are there any changes for you to make?

Be specific and write on the back of your drawing the steps that you will need to take to effect the necessary changes. Make sure that they are manageable and not unrealistic.

When you have finished, spend some time with your heavenly Father, whom Jesus likened to the gardener (John 15:1, NIV), the one who knows you better than you know yourself and loves you with an unconditional, life-giving love. Commit your way to him and let him guide you in the days ahead.

Keep your drawing and refer to it in a few years' time, noting the changes as life moves on.

poem

JOYCE HUGGETT

Embracing God's World

author

Joyce Huggett is a well-known Christian author of bestselling books on listening to God. She is now based in the UK after years serving overseas.

These poems are taken from *Embracing God's World: prayers for the yearning heart*, BRF, 2007, a selection of prayers old and new made by Joyce Huggett.

Love rekindled

I'm sitting in the forest
hurting,
burdened,
questioning.
Two great-tits come to visit.
They hop on to the branch of the great pine
under whose branches
I'm sheltering from the sun.
They sit.
They sing.
They disappear.

'I know when one such fledgling falls,'
you whisper.
'And you are more precious to me
than the smallest sparrow.'

I marvel.
You know me through and through,
yet I matter to you.

I transfer to you afresh
the burden of my unanswered questions
and my love for you is rekindled.

Thank you

MAGGIE ROSS

Cranberries

In this extract taken from her book *Writing the Icon of the Heart* (BRF, 2011) Maggie Ross writes from her experience of praying in wild places where cranberries are to be found...

... close enough to touch

author

Maggie Ross is the pseudonym of a professed Anglican solitary, who divides her time between Oxford and the USA, preaching, lecturing, leading retreats, offering pastoral care, and writing books and liturgies.

Moses did not know that the skin of his face shone because he had been talking with God.
EXODUS 34:29

September in the heart of Denali, just outside the border of the national park near the old mining town of Kantishna: the silent land is expectant. The first blanket of snow could come at any time. The tundra is suffused with the slanting light of a lingering sun; the heavy golden air is filigreed with the hoarse fluting of cranes as they spiral to the heavens. The mountain's presence is tactile. Wickersham Wall, the 15,000-foot expanse of sheer grey granite, seems close enough to touch, though it is 30 miles away as the raven flies, across a landscape saturated with autumn, soaked with the radiance of cranberries.

Cranberries: low-bush cranberries, to be specific. Easily over-looked, trodden underfoot, they spring back from their bed of Labrador tea, unbruised and unhurt. Growing with blueberries and crowberries, they provide some of the loveliest patterns of colour in nature. When half-ripe they are brilliant scarlet against the blue-silver of new spruce growth, the russet of bearberry or the grey of reindeer lichen; their brilliant hues hint of Christmas. As the cranberries ripen, their scarlet transmutes into a darker purple-red; they become harder to find. Once made brilliant by bright sun, their subdued maturity is now made visible in the more subtle light of high clouds or the sheen of mist and rain.

Cranberries. I've been living with cranberries for a week now, gallons of them. To be out in the vastness amid their prodigal abundance makes me glad I have to pick them on my knees. I go out with my backpack, some gallon jugs and the berry rake. When I find patches where berries grow thick enough to use it, I feel rather like a small bear, clawing with my wooden paw through the vegetation, putting the harvest into containers instead of my mouth. Slowly

As the cranberries ripen, their scarlet transmutes into a darker purple-red; they become **harder to find...**

the jars fill, and slowly my backpack becomes heavier.

Late one sunny afternoon I brought my haul back to camp, rolling the cranberries by handfuls down an inclined frame on which a piece of woollen blanket had been stretched, the rough cloth catching the bits of leaf and moss that inevitably are picked with the berries. They rattled on to a flat tray, the crimson punctuated by the odd blueberry or crowberry.

I feel rather like a small bear, clawing with my wooden paw through the vegetation...

... the angled light made the berries glow ever **more deeply from within**

When the tray was full, I looked at it as if for the first time and caught my breath. A phrase from Psalm 34 leapt to mind, 'Look on me and be radiant...' (v. 5). I picked up the tray of radiance and set it on the bench outside the food storage cache where the angled light made the berries glow ever more deeply from within.

This same radiance extends to everyone at our camp, guest or staff, no matter what the weather; it shines from their faces. They arrive tired and stressed, travel-weary, even a little suspicious if they are first-timers, not knowing quite what they will find in the people or the wilderness. But soon the quiet magic of the land takes hold: a caribou against the horizon; a bear cavorting among the willow; a wolf at its kill; tiny spring flowers still to be found among the few snow patches remaining from last winter; a pair of ravens soaring overhead, calling, calling; the cloudy drape drawing back from The Mountain to reveal its glory.

This glory of cranberries and wilderness bestows humility in the radiance that captures us and is reflected in our faces. It is most present when we are least self-conscious, when our awareness is focused outside ourselves and we are briefly taken into a space where the ordinary preoccupations of time are laid aside. Above all, it is a gift, as the cranberries themselves are a gift. This radiance is the trace of divine love that creates and sustains, lingering in all creation, no matter how muted it may seem. The ability to see this love depends on our receptivity to the gift of humility, which is contemplation, purity of heart and peace all rolled into one, the single virtue of which the paradoxes of the Beatitudes speak.

Put more simply, only love can recognise Love. It is only because we bear, each one of us, each fragment of creation, the trace of the divine that we dimly recognise, that the hunger crying out from every human heart can be fed by this radiance alone.

It is these commonplace cranberry events that underlie the wisdom of the Judeo-Christian heritage. The psalms are full of such references. God needs mere fingers to make the heavens, the stars and the moon (Psalm 8:4); he sports with Leviathan (104:28) and feeds the young ravens when they cry (147:10). The psalms refer not only to the natural world but also to the profound effect that world has on us, what it reveals of our psychology and character. The phrase from Psalm 34 is an example: look on me and be radiant, and let not

This glory of cranberries and wilderness bestows humility in the radiance that captures us and is reflected in our faces. It is most present when we are least self-conscious, when our awareness is focused outside ourselves...

your faces be ashamed (v. 5).

For in the light of this radiance, all else is forgotten, all that preoccupies and troubles us, all our pain and dismay. It is not that they are excised or erased but, as the contemporary philosopher Erazim Kohàk has remarked, our pain becomes part of something larger than ourselves, and is transfigured. In his book *An Evil Cradling*, a modern *Dark Night of the Soul*, Brian Keenan describes the moment when, in the midst of despair induced by solitary confinement, he was given an orange. Starved as he was for fresh fruit, he could not bear to eat it but could only behold the wonder of its colour, its form, its radiance in the dark.

> ... Our pain becomes part of something larger than ourselves, and is transfigured

Through these transfigurations, we realise concretely what the ancients knew—our participation in the divine nature. We are with Moses and the elders, whose beholding on the mountain and its effects constitutes one of the biblical passages most frequently cited by contemplative writers. This same beholding is promised to all of us, as summed up in the sublime vision of Revelation:

Then the angel showed me the river of the water of life, bright as crystal, flowing from the throne of God and of the Lamb through the middle of the street of the city. On either side of the river is the tree of life with its twelve kinds of fruit, producing its fruit each month; and the leaves of the tree are for the healing of the nations. Nothing accursed will be found there any more. But the throne of God and of the Lamb will be in it, and his servants will worship him; they will see his face, and his name will be on their foreheads. And there will be no more night; they need no light of lamp or sun, for the Lord God will be their light, and they will reign for ever and ever. (Revelation 22:1–5)

Our seeking into the beholding is not a matter of rejecting the particularities of creation but rather plunging into their deepest heart, allowing them wholly to draw our attention. '*Amor meus, pondus meum*,' said St Augustine. Love draws everything to itself, and this radiant love is the source of all fruitfulness.

My Space

This space is for you to make your own notes.

A place to pause on the journey, look at the view and anticipate the next step

Quiet Spaces subscriptions

Quiet Spaces is published three times a year, in May, September and January. To take out a subscription, please complete this form, indicating the month in which you would like your subscription to begin.

❏ I would like to take out a subscription myself

Name ______________________________

Address ______________________________

Postcode __________ Telephone Number ______________________________

Email ______________________________

❏ Please do not send me further information about BRF publications.

❏ I would like to give a gift subscription (please complete your name and address above and details of the person you want to give a subscription to below)

Gift subscription name ______________________________

Gift subscription address ______________________________

____

______________________________ Postcode __________

Please send beginning with the Jan 12 / May 12 / Sep 12 issue: (delete as applicable)

(please tick box)	UK	SURFACE	AIRMAIL
Quiet Spaces	❏ £16.95	❏ £19.05	❏ £21.60

Please complete the payment details below and send this coupon, with payment to: BRF, 15 The Chambers, Vineyard, Abingdon OX14 3FE.

Method: ❏ Cheque (payable to BRF) ❏ Mastercard ❏ Visa ❏ Maestro

Card no. ❏❏❏❏❏❏❏❏❏❏❏❏❏❏❏❏❏❏❏

Valid from ❏❏❏❏ Expires ❏❏❏❏ Issue no. of Maestro card ❏❏❏

Security Code ❏❏❏

Signature ______________________________ Date ____ / ____ / ____

All orders must be accompanied by the appropriate payment.

PROMO REF: QSSIT

To order *Quiet Spaces* or other BRF publications mentioned in this journal, visit your local Christian bookshop or go to BRF's website www.brfonline.org.uk.